Secrets of Wine Tasting

The Ultimate Guide To Learn Everything About Wine Tasting & Wine Selecting

Copyright 2015 by Better Life Solutions- All rights reserved.

This document is geared towards providing exact and reliable information in regards to the topic and issue covered. The publication is sold with the idea that the publisher is not required to render accounting, officially permitted, or otherwise, qualified services. If advice is necessary, legal or professional, a practiced individual in the profession should be ordered.

- From a Declaration of Principles which was accepted and approved equally by a Committee of the American Bar Association and a Committee of Publishers and Associations.

In no way is it legal to reproduce, duplicate, or transmit any part of this document in either electronic means or in printed format. Recording of this publication is strictly prohibited and any storage of this document is not allowed unless with written permission from the publisher. All rights reserved.

The information provided herein is stated to be truthful and consistent, in that any liability, in terms of inattention or otherwise, by any usage or abuse of any policies, processes, or directions contained within is the solitary and utter responsibility of the recipient reader. Under no circumstances will any legal responsibility or blame be held against the publisher for any reparation, damages, or monetary loss due to the information herein, either directly or indirectly.

Respective authors own all copyrights not held by the publisher.

The information herein is offered for informational purposes solely, and is universal as so. The presentation of the information is without contract or any type of guarantee assurance.

The trademarks that are used are without any consent, and the publication of the trademark is without permission or backing by the trademark owner. All trademarks and brands within this book are for clarifying purposes only and are the owned by the owners themselves, not affiliated with this document.

Table of Contents

Introduction 4

About Wine 5

The Unique Experience of Wine Tasting 17

Wine Assessment 23

The Amazing Connection between Wine and Food 26

The Elusive Flavors and Aromas of Wine 36

Grape Varieties 41

Wine Varieties 44

How to Choose the Perfect Wine for Every Occasion 47

Did You Know? 53

Introduction

This book contains proven steps and strategies on how to taste and select wine.

Apart from that, you will have the opportunity to discover inside information about the world of wine tasting. Based on the information presented in this book, you will soon become a wine expert, being able to recommend the finest wines to others.

Here Is A Preview Of What You'll Learn...

- Wine tasting basics – sight, smell, taste
- Wine assessment procedure
- The information provided by the color, smell and taste of the wine
- Pairing the right wine with the right food
- Rules about choosing a particular wine for a dinner menu
- Wine flavors and aromas
- Grape and wine varieties from all over the world
- How to choose the perfect wine for every occasion

And much, much more!

About Wine

Wine is the favorite alcoholic beverage for millions of people around the world. Some of them like it for its taste, some for the feeling they get after drinking it. However, those who don't know the complex history of this noble

drink don't appreciate it as those who do. Once you realize

that wine followed humans throughout the history and it can be said that it is one of the most important traits of human civilization. You might think this is not true, but as soon as you finish reading this book, you will start thinking otherwise.

The roots of wine production most likely originate from ancient Persia. Egyptians, Phoenicians, Greeks and Romans loved strong, full wines with high alcohol content, which they had to dilute with water. In the Bible, the wine is mentioned 521 times. Dionysus in Greece and Bacchus in Rome were the gods of wine. Since ancient times, the power of wine to exalt man, to give them serenity and the gift of speech, made wine, in the eyes of the people, appear as a drink of the gods. People loved to peek into the world of divine drinks and wine often opened the way to women's hearts. However, with wine glass, wars also used to be declared. Wine was used to celebrate the birth, marked a success, but it is not just a drink of joy, because it was also drank at funerals. Wine was and still is an appreciated drink for many civilizations. You could say that anything goes, just good wine remains.

One Frenchman said: "All the fashion pass, only wine remains". Undoubtedly, the wine represents the most civilized and the most cultivated mean of enjoyment and a cultural and civilization challenge. True wine culture as, indeed, any other, is acquired over time and involves, mainly, certain knowledge of the grapevines, of its occurrence in the country and in the region, knowledge of basic production of certain types of wine, ways of storing wine, serving wine, reading labels, understanding the temperature of wine, stacking wine and food, etc. Wine culture also includes knowledge about wine and aesthetics, art and wine, and wine and health.

In general culture of a person or even a whole nation, the knowledge of serving beverages, is included. If this applies to serving and serving wine then there is a special term "wine culture". It actually implies groomed, sophisticated or civilized consumption of this drink. Wine culture is not measured by quantities of consumed wine, but it's rather an adoption of certain knowledge and procedures in the field of viticulture, oenology and gastronomy. This includes a vocabulary needed to describe the sensory characteristics of the wine and knowledge of the role of wine in the modern business world. It is particularly important to inform the public about the positive effects of drinking moderate amounts of wine on one's health. Also people should get to know about how the wine can improve the gastronomic experience and overall mood at the table.

Wine is an integral and inseparable part of European life and culture. The European Union is the largest wine producer in the world, as well as leading exporter of wine and wine products in the world. The wine sector contributes around 15 billion Euros a year to the economies of EU countries. The importance of the wine sector in the economies of European countries, however, should not be counted only in money. Wine sector permeates many levels of European life, contributes significantly to society in socio-economic, environmental and social conditions: vines and vineyards dot the landscape, the wine sector provides employment to millions of people, helping to maintain the thread of rural societies and maintaining the way of life that is central the very notion of European identity. Not least, wine and wine products have enjoyed a long history, and are now enjoyed by millions of people in Europe and around the world. The countries in Europe that are considered to produce the best wine are France, Spain, Italy, Portugal, and Germany. Outside of Europe, the great wine can be found in the United States (California), Argentina, Chile, South Africa, Australia, etc.

Wine and wine culture has become an essential part of European life, culture and diet, since the time immemorial. Technology of production of wine appeared in Europe with the expansion of the Roman Empire to the Mediterranean. Then they established many large producers of wine in the areas which still today remain as wine heavens. Even then, the wine production process was fairly precisely defined, and farms that dealt with growing vines had formed techniques for different grape varieties. First appeared barrels for storage and transport of wine, then a glass bottle, even a rudimentary system of tags was developed in individual regions and as such very quickly gained a reputation for the classification of "fine wine." As the wine production progressively improved, its popularity increased and wine taverns became a common feature in cities throughout the Roman Empire.

The culture of wine consuming in Europe did not start in Rome. Ancient Greeks preceded the Romans: wine inspired poets, historians and artists of the era. In Greece, however, wine was considered a privilege for the upper classes. Dionysus, the Greek god of wine, was presented not only through the intoxicating power of wine, but also through its social and beneficial influences. Greeks looked at the wine god as the promoter of civilization, legislator, and a lover of peace. Dionysus was also worshiped as the patron deity of agriculture and theater. Indeed, according to the ancient Greek historian Thucydides, "the peoples of the Mediterranean began to emerge from barbarism when they learned the ability to cultivate olives and wine."

How the time passed, the art of wine production spread to France, Spain, Germany and parts of Britain. By the time, wine was considered an important part of daily diet and people began to favor stronger, heavier wines. European appreciation of remained the same during the Middle Ages. Partly because drinking water was still unreliable for reasons of hygiene, and the wine was the preferred drink to accompany meals. At the same time, viticulture and wine making were progressing during that period, thanks to the agricultural orientation of the churches and monasteries across the European continent. That gave rise to the development of some of the finest vineyards in Europe. The Benedictine monks, for example, were numbered among Europe's largest wine producers with vineyards in France's Champagne, Burgundy and Bordeaux region, as well as Rajngou and Franconia in Germany. Merchants and people from the noble classes of the time had wine with every meal and maintained a well-stocked wine cellar.

During the 16th century, wine became appreciated as a more sophisticated alternative to beer and as production began to diversify, the consumers have begun to change their habits according to the concept of value. People began to talk about the virtues and vices of wine with greater vigor than in previous centuries. Shakespeare remarked that "good wine is a good familiar creature if it is well used", implicitly commenting on the misuse of wine at the moment. Shakespeare's era suffered the availability of fresh drinking water in London, which certainly had an impact on the wine industry of that era.

Improved production techniques in the 17th and 18th centuries led to the emergence of a finer quality wine. In this period, people began to use glass bottles with plugs, and thus invented the corkscrew – the same that exists today. French wine industry has experienced the upswing at that moment, with special recognition received by the Bordeaux region from the merchants from the Netherlands, Germany, Ireland and Scandinavia. Bordeaux traded wine for coffee and other requested foods from the New World, helping to cement the role of the emerging global wine trade.

Although the 19th century is considered the golden age of wine for many regions, it wasn't without problems. Around 1863, many French vines suffered from a disease caused by phylloxera, which is sucking the juice from the root of the plant. When it was discovered that vines in America were resistant to phylloxera it was decided to plant American vines clones in the affected French regions. This has created the application of hybrid varieties of grapes that give a greater variety of wines. Also, at this time French winemakers moved en masse to the Rioja region of northern Spain and taught local people to produce wine from local grape varieties.

Over the last 150 years, the winemaking technology has undergone a complete revolution, same as art and science. With the invention of cooling devices, it became easy for wineries to control the temperature of fermentation and produce high quality wines in hot climates. Although the wine industry faces the challenge of meeting the constantly increasing demands of the market, without losing the individual character of its wines, the technology helps them to ensure a consistent supply of quality wines. The modern level of quality wine pays homage and gratitude to the timeless art of wine-making which established the modern technologies. It points to the importance of wine in the history and diversity of the European culture.

Wine is a very complex drink, with over 600 chemical compounds in its composition, some of which were just recently detected and quantified. Most of these components in wine are in very small quantities, but they have an important role in the taste and aroma of wine. The value of wine from hygienic and nutritional point of view, was what **interested** people for centuries. That is why they defined wine in different ways. For some, wine is an alcoholic beverage, for others it's food or medicine. The interpretation that the wine is not food, as it does not contain enough essential fatty acids, vitamins, and protein, is not convincing because sugar, oil, and other similar foods, do not include these important elements as well.

The biggest problem about often consumption of wine is a high alcohol content (ethanol). It is well known that the alcohol introduced into the body quickly diffuses through the walls of the stomach and intestines, leads to the liver and enters the blood stream. From the blood, alcohol disappears for 12 hours, but stays in the tissue for 16 more hours. If the wine is consumed with food, alcohol levels are lower than if the wine was consumed only. The alcohol is eliminated from the organism through the lungs (0.5 - 1% of the amount of the entered if a person is at rest, and 5 - 10%

if it is active), the kidneys (20 - 30%) and biochemical transformations in the liver.

Small amounts of alcohol ingested into the human body will activate the salivary glands and make the stomach secrete the gastric juice. Larger quantities have a negative impact on the wall of the stomach, increase the blood pressure, cause rapid heart rate and an increase in the peripheral temperature. It was also proved that the alcohol in wine is far less toxic than the same amount of alcohol in spirit drinks. That is how the hypothesis that the wine contains substances that alleviate effects of alcohol, was created. This property is attributed to phenolic substances in wine. Certainly, when we talk about the health aspects of wine, then we think of the moderate consumption. On this question the best answer was given by Parazelzus: "Only the quantity makes one thing a poison or a cure."

Regarding the medicinal properties of wine, they are known since the ancient times. Pasteur was the first to say that wine is the healthiest and most hygienic drink in the world. Wine in its composition contains minerals, acids, vitamin A, and particularly important phenolic compounds (proantocianidoli), which is known to have an extremely positive effect. Since 1991, it's debated about the so-called French paradox, underlined by the fact that the French consume a lot of fat of animal origin, but have a much smaller number of myocardial infarction in relation to the Americans and other nations of Western Europe. Substances that have antioxidant effects such as proanthocyanidins, quercetin and reservartrol (phenolic compounds), which are especially prevalent in red wine, have a role as a coronary patron. These compounds inhibit the oxidation of LDL, on the other hand, they increase the high density lipoprotein - HDL levels, which are considered to be positive regulators of fat in the blood. The wine was found to have around 60 mg / l of salicylic acid, which is the double the amount of the daily dose of aspirin, which physicians recommend as prevention for cardiovascular diseases.

In addition to these properties, the wine also has strong anti-bacteria properties, known since ancient times. In 1892, Alois Pick poisoned water with bacteria that causes cholera, mixed it with 1/3 wine and after 5 minutes he drank it, without any consequences for his health. The bactericidal effect of wine is attributed to many compounds – acids, alcohol, etc, but the greatest impact on it, have phenolic compounds. Finally, it should be noted that all of these properties of wine were confirmed in practice. French League against Cancer published data which shows that the population of wine-growing regions is far less to die of malignant disease than people in other parts of the country. It was found that in the wine-growing areas of France, there are almost two times more octogenarians than in regions where wine culture is not on a high level.

The Unique Experience of Wine Tasting

In order to discover a wine and all of its qualities, one must not only taste but also see and smell this wonderful liquor. The first thing that you must start with is assess how clear the wine actually is. Cloudy wines are not acceptable for tasting, so they have to be discarded and a new glass poured. The flow of the wine should also be appreciated; for this part of the process, you will need to take the glass of wine and perform a few gentle swirls.

Depending on the alcohol content of the wine, you will see more or less threads of wine running down the glass. According to the experts in the field, the higher the alcohol content of the analyzed wine, the fewer threads you will see on the glass.

Apart from the clearness and flow, one must analyze the color of the wine. It is recommended that this observation is made in natural light, as the artificial one is known to modify your perception of the actual color of the wine (for example, you will probably see a red wine to be brown in color).

Generally speaking, the red wines vary from light rose to darker tones. In fact, there are certain varieties of wine that appear to be black, due to their increased opacity. White wines have varied colors as well, ranging from white to rich gold tones. It should be mentioned that rose wines are only rarely pink in color. As a matter of fact, they exhibit a wonderful blend between pink and other colors, such as blue, purple or orange.

There are a number of factors that influence the color of a wine, starting with the type of grapes (white or red), how ripe the grapes actually are and in which district they were produced. Moreover, the color of a wine is influenced by the chosen method to produce the actual wine, not to mention the age of the wine.

Once you have assessed the color of the wine, it is the perfect time to move on to the smelling part. You should start by swirling the wine gently in the glass, placing your smelling equipment inside the glass and inhaling deeply. The olfactory bulb is responsible for helping you identify the flavors of the wine; the more often you repeat the smelling of the same wine, the more accustomed you will become to the flavors, missing out on the existing subtleties. This is why it is for the best that you let at least two minutes pass before smelling the same wine; or, if you want, you can smell another wine in the meantime.

The actual tasting of the wine is the most rewarding experience, as it delivers information about a particular wine in a direct manner. If you want to discover the wine in its entire splendor, be sure to take a big gulp of wine and try to draw air through the wine. You might be a little embarrassed at first by the sounds that come out but it will be all worth it, as you will be able to identify all of the characteristics of the wine, in the back of the throat.

There are a few simple things that you need to remember in order to start off your wine-tasting career. No one is born a professional, everything has a start and the same is with wine tasting. That is why you need to go over these few rules and to build the knowledge based on this.

1. Temperature

In the case of white wine, it is necessary to cool the bottle in the fridge for an hour before use, unless, you are planning to use it as something else. Then it really does not matter, because all wine experts would say that mixing water and wine is a sort of blasphemy. So, if you are not planning a blasphemous act, cool the wine for about an hour before bringing it to the table. Red wines are served at room temperature. But, that does not mean that the temperature should be hot in the summer and colder in the winter – it

has to be somewhere between 18 ° C and 23 ° C.

2. Wine opening

Once you open the bottle, take a look at the cork, checking that there are no traces of cracking. Smell it to check whether the plug is in good condition and there is no mold. If it is present on the upper side is not particularly a big deal - just wipe before you thrust the opener. But if it's on the

bottom side, be careful. And do not think that if you take a good wine this will not happen. One more thing, make sure that the pieces of the cork did not break into the wine while you were opening it.

3. Wine breathing

Once you have opened a bottle of wine it is necessary to allow it to "breathe". Again, in other words: to let some substances in wine get settled down to give it its full bouquet, it is necessary for the wine to be in the contact with air for a while. In many cases, white wine can be drunk immediately after the opening, while the black takes up to several hours. Experts generally use the time range between one hour and three hours.

4. Holding the glass.

This mainly serves for you to impress your guests, if you're an amateur, while if you have a quite a lot of experience in wine tasting, you will see that the way you hold the glass can make a big impact on the wine's taste. The golden rule is that you should be holding the cup by the neck and not by the body. Why? In addition to being aesthetically more beautiful and elegant, from a practical side, it does not cover your view of the wine. Also you will not heat up the wine with the temperature of your hands. Be careful not to overfill the cup while pouring, it's as ugly as is impractical.

5. Drinking

The basic principles are: smell the wine - if you like the smell, the wine is good; look at the wine - if the color is and beautiful, it's good; taste it - if you like it, it's a good wine.

Wine Assessment

If you want to form a correct opinion in regard to a certain wine, you have to go through all the above mentioned steps. It is for the best not to come to any conclusions until you have seen, smelled and tasted the wine. A sample tasting should provide you with all the information you need and each stage of the process should be used in order to confirm the information gathered from the previous one. Learn to have confidence in your own opinion and do not let yourself be influenced by the opinion of other people.

The Socratic Method is perfect for a complex wine assessment; you can ask questions about different features of the wine and rely on your own judgment in order to obtain the answer. Let us take the color of the wine, for example. You can take a good look at the wine in the glass, assessing whether the color is a deep or a pale shade. The color can offer a lot of information about the wine; depending on the color, you can actually tell the age of the wine. Allow your visual senses to go beyond their limit and try to remember if the wine reminds you of a particular variety, vineyard you have visited or other things like that. Last, but not least, check out how intense the color at the rim of the glass actually is. This will also provide useful information about the quality of the wine (the more intense, the higher the quality).

Continue with the same method when you are assessing the smell of the wine. Use your fine sense of smell in order to determine if the wine has a distinctive aroma or if it is rather bland. The smell of the wine can also provide information about its age, a person being able to tell the difference between youthful and mature wines. However, there are certain wines that are difficult to distinguish, requiring more years of experience in the field of wine tasting. If you have recently discovered this passion, it is for the best to stick with wines that have easy-to-recognize features. Through the smell, you can also determine whether a wine is ready to be drunk or not. The detection of vanilla or toffee notes is significant of the wine having aged in oak barrels.

In the world of wine tasting, it is said that the taste of a wine should reflect the information you have obtained by smelling it. While this might be more difficult at first, you have to put your trust into your own palate and allow it to detect the level of acidity or sweetness a wine actually possesses. Through the careful tasting process, you can also determine the alcoholic strength of the wine. The taste of a red wine is given by the tanning content; this is given by the maceration of the grape juice together with the skin (the longer the maceration, the higher tanning content the wine will possess). A high content of tannin is encountered in aged wines and you will certainly notice the differences by drinking a youthful one. On the other hand, by tasting a sparkling wine, you will have to take into consideration certain characteristics of the bubbles. For example, it is said that high quality wines have bubbles that are smaller in size.

The Amazing Connection between Wine and Food

There is no secret that wine and food share a deep and intimate connection, bringing each other's flavors to the light. Experts recommended that the wine should be chosen in accordance to the flavors of the prepared dish; delicate wines go perfect with delicate dishes, while highly flavored wines are more recommended for stronger dishes. There are also other rules that you have to follow in terms of wine etiquette when serving a several-courses menu. First of all, the white wine is always served before the red variety. Then, you must serve the dry before the sweet and the light before the heavier. Last, but not least, the youthful varieties have to be included in the earlier dishes, the old ones being recommended for the last courses.

If you are planning an entire menu course, you might be tempted to choose a wine from a different country or region for each dish. This is actually not something that you want to do; according to the experts in the field, it is for the best that you stick with the same variety, country or region throughout the entire menu. You can choose any kind of wine you want but make sure that you are consistent with the above mentioned rule.

Wines have been used as aperitifs for a long time now, this being a common custom in the region of France (Sauternes are often offered as an aperitif, at the start of a meal). Whether you decide to prepare a simple menu or you want to succeed at a several-course dinner, it is important to choose the right wines to be offered as aperitifs. White wines are highly recommended for such purposes, especially those that are light and dry; however, both still and sparkling white wines can be given at the start of a meal. Among the most recommended white wines as aperitifs, there are: Mâcon Blanc, Mâcon Villages, Muscadet, Alsace wines (Pinot Blanc), Chardonnay and Sauvignon. The most excellent and delicious aperitif remains the famous Champagne.

Each appetizer that you plan on serving will suit wonderfully to a certain selection of wines. The buttered artichokes are best enjoyed with a delicious yet dry Sauvignon Blanc, while artichokes in Hollandaise sauce can be served with a dry wine from the Loire valley of France. Appetizers with asparagus are even more amazing when one serves a glass of Champagne or one of the famous Alsace wines (Muscat d'Alsace, for example). Your avocado appetizers can be easily paired with a beautiful Alsace Gewürztraminer, being especially recommended on account of its reduced acidity. If you are looking for a classic combination, you will definitely consider pairing the tasty caviar with a chilled glass of Champagne.

The acidity of the wine is an important element to consider when pairing food with wine. For example, if you have prepared garlic butter, a wine with a higher acidity is much more recommended that one with a low acidity. The classic and elegant Champagne is perfect not only for caviar but also for deluxe pates such as foie gras. Dry white wines, such as Muscadet, are recommended for plain green salads, while Champagne appears once more as a classic choice for salads that contain warm ingredients. Both red and white wines from the Burgundy region work fine for appetizers that have snails as main ingredient. If you are serving soups as appetizers, you can choose the elegant Champagne for cream soups and a Bordeaux or Burgundy variety for game soup. Egg and pasta dishes are more delicious when served with sparkling Champagne.

If you plan on including fish or shellfish in your menu, the most obvious choice in terms of wine is represented by a dry white variety. Intensely flavored wines, such as the varieties from the Loire valley of France, are recommended for fish dishes that have sauces or for those that have been cooked in the frying pan. Despite the fact that white wine is most often recommended for fish, there are certain fish dishes that work with red wine as well. A particular example is the fish stew, the red wine being added as an ingredient to the dish. If you are cooking mackerel, the best wine to serve to this dish is a Sauvignon from the Loire valley. On the other hand, if you are planning on serving smoked fish, you should consider a wine that is richer in flavor. Experts recommended that you follow a specific rule when choosing the wine for smoked fish; the rule is that oaked wine goes perfect with anything that is smoked (oaked Chardonnay, for example).

When it comes to river fish, the choice of wine to pair the dish with depends on the actual type of fish. The all-purpose choice for dishes with river fish is the rose wine but more specific choices include Champagne for pike or salmon and Alsace or German Riesling for trout. A delicate choice for sardine dishes is represented by a Portuguese wine, known by the name of Vinho Verde. Shellfish also works great with wine, the most recommended choices being: Muscadet (shrimp, mussels), Sancerre (crayfish) and Champagne (crab, lobster or oysters). White fish has a light flavor, so light-bodied and youthful Champagne wines are the perfect choice for such a dish.

As for meat, the general rule says that red wines go with dark meat, while white wines go with light meat. Once you accumulate knowledge and experience about wines, you can skip this rule and choose the wine according to the flavors that you bring to the light in your dish. Beef dishes are often paired with red wine; for example, you can serve a delicious roast beef with delicate Bordeaux wine, reserving a more youthful variety, such as Côtes-du-Rhône for beef burgers.

The choice of wine for casserole dishes also depends on the type of meat that was used; if you casserole has dark meat, you need a red wine that is rich in flavor, such as those from the Bordeaux or Burgundy region. On the other hand, if you are serving a casserole with light meat, you can either choose a youthful red wine from the Loire Valley of France or a delicate white, such as Mâcon Blanc.

International dishes, such as those borrowed from the Chinese cuisine, are best served with a rich Riesling from German regions or a demi-sec variety in case they also contain duck or goose. If you are serving duck with orange sauce, you can consider pairing this dish with a red or white one, those from the Burgundy region being the most recommended. Pheasant is even more delicious when you serve it with a rich-flavored red wine from the Bordeaux or Burgundy region. On the other hand, if you are serving good, you can choose a red Chianti or Chinon or re-direct your attention to the white varieties, such as Riesling or Champagne.

Traditional dishes, such as goulash, are best served with full-bodied wines that are produced in the same region, such as those from Eastern Europe. Red wine is also a perfect recommendation for Indian dishes, especially the lighter varieties. Bordeaux wines and lamb represent a classic combination, while red wines from the Alsace or Germany regions are generally recommended for dishes that have pork, poultry or veal as ingredients.

Wine can be served for dessert as well, enhancing their sweet and delicious flavors. For example, the Tokaji wine variety is recommended to be served with cakes, puddings and pastries. A Pinot from the Alsace region is suitable for a sweet and luxurious desert such as crème brûlée. On the other hand, when it comes to fruits, ripe peaches are best served with a light Riesling, while the fruit salad is best combined with light-bodied Sauternes. If you are a fine of strawberries, you can make a killer combination by adding a glass of Gewürztraminer. Muscat varieties are recommended for desserts that include ice cream, whereas the sparkling Moscato is best served with meringue desserts.

If you are planning on serving a platter of cheeses, there are several wines you can consider for the perfect combination. Port wines are often recommended blue cheeses but you can also choose Alsace or Gewürztraminer wine varieties. For semi-soft cheeses, you can easily add an elegant glass of Pinot Noir from the Alsace region; whereas, for the semi-strong cheeses, it is recommended that you select a strong Gewürztraminer. Hard cheeses are best served with a fine wine from the Bordeaux region, while goat cheese is recommended to be associated with a dry white wine, eventually from the Gewürztraminer variety.

When it comes to wine serving there are many things people are concerned with. Knowing how to fit the wine with the chosen food and vice versa, can sometimes pose a big problem. The first reason is that some foods just don't go well with certain types of wine. The other, more often, problem is of social nature. Wine drinking has its rules, which have been there for at least a couple of centuries. So in order not to seem ignorant in front of your friends, or to appear ill-mannered in a restaurant, you need to learn which wines go with which food and the other way around.

There are two ways of serving - wine along with food or food with wine? It is depending on the situation in which we are. In the first, we try to make a certain food match the wine. In the second, we need to choose the appropriate wine for the food served to us. Due to such a difficult task, a good advice and some education are needed. So, here are a couple of examples. Remember these and you will never have problems with stacking your wine with your meals, ever again.

• Greek Samian wine: spicy food, salads, grilled vegetables, fish (including smoked fish).

• Sauvignon blanc: seafood, Thai food, goat cheese, salads, vegetables (except mushrooms), fried fish, spicy sauces.

• Chardonnay: almost every type of fish (other than those greasiest), from oysters to richly flavored fish dishes and stews, fatty cheeses.

• Pinot blanc: fish, batter with vegetables, fish stew or fish soup, risotto, pastry with creamy sauces, chicken.

• Cabernet Sauvignon and Merlot: red meat, sausages, meat and grilled vegetables, meat from wild animals.

• Pinot noir: salmon, tuna, mushrooms, pork, duck, quail, everything made from beans, partridge.

• Shiraz wine: roast turkey, goose, duck, sausages, meat and grilled vegetables, cooked dishes with meat and vegetables, meat from wild animals.

The Elusive Flavors and Aromas of Wine

As a wine taster, you will often confront with subtle flavors and aromas, trying hard to identify them. It is important to remember that some flavors are more pregnant than others, while many just add to the complexities of the wine. In some cases, the flavors are actually signs that the wine is faulty. Also, it should be mentioned that the flavors identified in the wine do not actually come from the wine containing fruits, vegetables or certain herbs. In the majority of the situations, they are a result of a chemical reaction, the process of vinification or of the barrels in which the wine was produced. It is perfectly acceptable to use fruity or flowers aromas in order to describe a certain wine.

Floral aromas are more commonly encountered in white wines that are young but also in red wines (violet is often identified as a strong aroma of such wines). The flowery aroma of acacia is seen in sparkling wines, while the elder flower is sometimes encountered in wine varieties that have been made from sparkling wine. Sweet wines can possess the aroma of geranium flowers, whereas the delicate scent of rose is encountered in Muscat and Gewürztraminer wines. Lavender is found in Australian Riesling and Muscat wines, in a wide variety of sparkling wines and sometimes in the German Riesling or Portuguese Vinho Verde. Violet is a distinct aroma of Cabernet red wines, such as those from the Bordeaux region; however, it should be mentioned that this is an aroma more often identified through the taste, rather than the scent.

A fruity aroma is an indication that the wine has been made from ripe grapes, being often more powerful in wines that are sweeter or more acidic. The apple flavor is commonly found in white wine: one can expect to encounter the green apple aroma in wines that are made from grapes that were not ripe enough, while the red apple flavor is suggestive of wines made from riper grapes. The apricot flavor is found in white wines from the Loire Valley or Germany, while the blackcurrant flavor is almost always encountered in Cabernet wines. The flavor of banana can be identified in both white and red wine; the first ones being cool-fermented, while the second one being made from carbonic maceration.

The red cherry flavor is characteristic of Pinot Noir, while the black cherry flavor is more common in fine Cabernet or Syrah wines. The dried fruit flavor, such as the one of the raisins, is often felt in the fortified Muscat wines. The fig flavor appears in combination with apple or melon, most commonly in young Chardonnay wines. Alsace wines, such as Gewürztraminer, have characteristic grapefruit aromas,

while lime is considered to be a distinct flavor of Australian Riesling wines. Young white wines have lemony flavors, while ripe Rieslings and Muscat wines have a powerful peach flavor. Melon is encountered as a flavor in young Chardonnay wines, while the flavor of strawberry is found in vintage Pinot Noir. When it comes to the orange flavor, there is a secret tip that you should know: this flavor is always found in Muscat wines but never in Gewürztraminer

ones. Also, the flavor of pear is found in both white and red wines.

There are different other aromas that you can discover in a wine, without being necessary related to flowers or fruits. For example, the butter aroma is characteristic of Chardonnay wines. The butterscotch aroma is frequently encountered in white wines that are fruity, being the result of the wines having aged in new oak. The caramel aroma is either encountered in young wines (as a mid-palate flavor) or in aged wines (as aftertaste). The chocolate aroma is characteristic for young, elegant wines, such as Cabernet Sauvignon or Pinot Noir. Coffee is one of the most interesting aromas to discover in a wine, this being often discovered in vintage Champagne. White wines that age have a beautiful honey aroma, such as the ones from the Burgundy region or any of the German Riesling varieties. The aroma of nuts you will find in aged Burgundy wines or in the classic Champagne (more common – walnuts or hazelnuts). The vanilla aroma is found in all wines that have aged in oak.

The vegetative or herbaceous flavors can add to the complexity of a wine but, in the majority of the situation, they represent signs that the respective wine is faulty. For example, the flavor of asparagus in a Sauvignon Blanc is a common indication that the wine has been made from grapes that are excessively ripe. On the other hand, the hay flavor is often encountered in sparkling wines, being an indication that the respective wine has gone through an oxidation process. The musty flavor of mushrooms is found in contaminated wines, as is the one of potato peelings (more common in red wines). When there is a chemical reaction, such as the one between ethyl alcohol and hydrogen sulphide, there is a very good chance to identify the onion or garlic flavor.

Grape Varieties

The grape variety is a determining factor in the taste of a wine, being influenced in its own turn by a series of other factors. Among these factors, there are: size of the grape, structure of the skin, skin color and thickness, acid and sugar content. According to the experts in the field, smaller grapes are the ones that deliver the highest concentration of flavor. Among the classic grape varieties with small fruits, you will find Cabernet Sauvignon and Riesling. This is not always the cases, as there are elegant wines, such as Pinot Noir, made from grape varieties with large fruits.

The structure of the skin is also important, as the grape skin contains a multitude of flavors. When determining the quality of a grape variety, experts take into consideration not only the construction but also the thickness of the grape skin. The Sauvignon Blanc wine is made from grapes that have a thicker skin; the aroma of this wine is influenced by the climate in which it is produced, including peach and gooseberry flavors. If such flavors are identified, this means that the wine has been made from ripe and thick-skinned grapes. However, one can also identify a hay or grass flavor, suggestive of grapes that were not ripe enough.

The color of the skin will also determine the color of the wine; for example, the skin of the Cabernet Sauvignon grape variety is dark in color, the wines resulting from it being dark-colored as well. On the other hand, the Merlot grape variety is light in color, which is why the wines resulting from it have a lighter color as well. The content of sugar in a grape will determine how much alcohol the wine will contain but also how sweet it will be. Experts bring together the sugar content and acidity of a wine in order to determine how balanced the wine actually is. Other factors that might have an influence over the grape variety include the climate (warm or cool), the soil and rootstock. However, it seems that the genetic inheritance of a grape variety will have a high power over the quality of the resulting wine.

Throughout the entire world, there are unbelievable grape varieties, each with its unique blend of flavors. Grape varieties have been blended, which led to the appearance of cross and hybrid species. In general, the white wines are made from grapes that range in color from amber to green (even though they are generically presented as white grapes), while red or rose wines are made from grapes that range in color from blue to black (these are known as black grapes). The interesting thing is that the white wines can also be made from black grapes (without the skin of the grape) but red wines are only made from black grapes. As you might have figured out by now, it is the pigment contained in the skin grape that gives the color of the wine. Also, the color of the wine is influenced by the acidity level.

Wine Varieties

Throughout the entire world, there are two main varieties of grapes, meaning white and red. The wines of France are regarded as the best in the world, the geography and climate playing a powerful role whereas their quality is concerned. The most classic wines from France include the ever sparkling Champagne, the luxurious red Burgundy and the rich, sweet Sauternes. In the region of Bordeaux, Merlot is considered the most important variety, while the region of Burgundy delivers some fines wines, such as Chardonnay and Pinot Noir. An excellent Pinot Noir is also made in the region of Côte de Nuits, while the region of Alsace is known

to produce white wines that are dry but rich in flavor. The Loire Valley is famous for the Sauvignon Blanc produced here; this is known as the only wine area in the entire world where Cabernet Franc is produced.

Italy has some fine wines as well, with the Moscato variety from Piedmont being renowned for its lightness and delicate sweetness. However, the region of Tuscany is most often associated with Italian wines, such as the traditional Chianti. Some pretty outstanding wines are made in the region of Emilia-Romagna, such as the classic Sangiovese Cabernet. In Spain, two of the most popular winemaking regions include Rioja (known for the oaky aroma of the wines) and Navarra. Portugal delivers Vinho Verde, one of the best dry wines in the world, the port variety from Douro Valley and the fortified wine of Madeira.

Germany impresses with its Riesling, Pinot Noir and Gewürztraminer varieties, while Austria has recently started to produce fine wines, such as Cabernet Sauvignon or Chardonnay. In Switzerland, the most famous variety is represented by Chasselas, whereas the wines of Luxembourg are among the finest of the entire north-western Europe. In the eastern part of Europe, one can easily fall in love with the Tokaji variety made in Hungary or with the delicate Pinot Noir of Romania.

The countries of Africa have started to produce excellent wines, the most popular varieties including Cabernet Sauvignon, Pinot Noir and Merlot. In America, excellent wines are produced in California and especially in the Napa Valley. Moving on to another continent, we can discover the creamy Shiraz variety from Australia and the fresh Sauvignon Blanc from New Zealand. Even Asia has started to be included as one of the top producers of wine in the world, with China providing an amazing Syrah variety.

How to Choose the Perfect Wine for Every Occasion

Choosing the perfect wine for a certain occasion is not easy, as there are so many great varieties to choose from. In general, it is said that that the white wines should be served during the early courses of a dinner or before the main course. This is because the white wines are light-bodied and drier than the red ones, being more suitable as aperitifs. Meals that are rich in taste or appetizers that have been made with creamy sauces work wonderfully with an elegant Chardonnay. On the other hand, if the early courses include salad, shrimp or fish, you can choose a fruity wine such as Sauvignon Blanc (not as dry as the Chardonnay wine variety). White wines can not only be used for early courses but also for toasts or special occasions, being commonly encountered in weddings (most often chosen – Chardonnay).

Red wines are more often reserved for the main courses, as they are full-bodied and perfect for a hearty meal. An ever-pleasing choice is represented by Merlot, especially for courses that include poultry, pork or lamb. For more special occasions, you can trust the elegant Pinot Noir varieties, seducing you with delicate plum notes and wonderful vanilla and blackberry flavors. If you are planning to include spicy foods in your menu, you can consider a wine such as Shiraz. This is because it has a peppery taste, enhancing the flavors of meat dishes and not only. Chianti on the other hand is recommended for tomato based dishes, fortified Port or Sauternes are among the finest dessert wines and Sangiovese wines bring out the flavors of simple, yet tasty spaghetti dishes.

Food is not the only thing to consider when choosing a wine for a particular occasion. You need to go beyond food pairing or the color of the wine. For example, you can take into consideration the crispness of a wine. A crisp wine will be selected just because of its acidic properties, being served at the start of a dinner (so as to stimulate the appetite). Sweet wines, on the other hand, have a high level of sugar and they work better with dishes that are blend in flavor. Remember: the sweetness of a wine is most often detected through the taste, not through the smell. Dry wines have a reduced sugar taste, being more often appreciated for their tanning taste. You can choose a dry wine for a meal that is already full of flavors, as this particular wine variety will not overwhelm your food.

The fruit aroma of fruity wines can be identified through both the smell and the taste. As opposed to dry wines, these contain reduced quantities of tannin and they have particular fruity notes that can be easily identified. These wines are either sweet and dry, with a wide array of fruity aromas, such as the one of strawberry or cherry. It is important to remember that both crisp and fruity wines do not age well, so it is for the best to drink them while they are still young. It is said that many of these wines will lose their flavor if let to age. Red wines have high tannin content, becoming more flavorful as they age.

Wine is there to beautify our life, not to make it more complicated. "We have to stop to evaluate the quality of wine" says Gary Vaynerchuk, the author of the book "101 Wines". As soon as we succeed in something like that, the sooner we will really be able to enjoy the wine. Following his advice, we present a few suggestions on how to make the most out of your next bottle of wine.

For the first date - wine which will help you be seductive needs to be strong, yet drinkable. You need something that you can grab from the table and take a right in the jacuzzi. We suggest Col Vetoras - Brut, made in Italy, because the real champagne (which comes only from France) has always been expensive. This sparkling extra dry white wine from Italy is an ideal replacement. It will awake the senses and make you relaxed.

For a dinner at sunset, we recommend Chateau de Fesles, Rose d'Anjou 'Le Jardin'. The country of origin is France and this rose wine is mild and sweet, and as such, is an ideal choice for serving with light summer meals and fruit treats. This is a wine with a fruity bouquet and a particularly strong scent of cherries. Alcohol content is not too big.

For a romantic dinner we recommend any kind of Pinot Noir from France. The smell of this wine is characterized by refined and balanced aromas of strawberry, berry, raspberry and moderate mineral spicy aromas. It makes it seductive and mysterious at the same time.

For fast food, we recommend several different kinds of wine. Improve the quality of food by going with sharper, more acidic wines. The price of these wines is slightly lower, but they will go very well with the fast food meal. With barbecue we suggest: Australian Merlot, because it is a rich, harmonious and varietal wine with high alcohol content. For this reason, it goes well with any red meat. The layered structure of this wine feels the taste of several ripe fruit flavors - wild fruit and berries.

With burrito, we suggest Cabernet Sauvignon. Forget the beer; turn the thirst off with this refreshing wine, which moderate sweetness goes well with spicy foods. Dominating taste of this wine is the fruity aroma of ripe cherries.

For a variety of pasta meals, we suggest: Sauvignon Blanc from Italy. Why? This is a wine that goes well with a wide range of dishes of Italian and Mediterranean cuisine. If you use your everyday table wine, you will not be disappointed, as well. The pleasant collage of spicy aromas and a hint of cherry will charm you.

Dinner for friends is the occasion when you need to offer a high-quality wine, perhaps from France as this country is considered the world's best when it comes to wine making.

We suggest French Chardonnay. This wine with a perfectly balanced sugar levels and acids will bring joy to the table. It will go perfect with any kind of meal that you want to prepare for your close friends. French Chardonnay has the aromas of green apples, pineapple bark, mild floral aroma, along with traces of citrus fruits, almond and creamy structure.

Did You Know?

The history of wine consumption is as long as human history, which is why it is no surprise there are many stories related to this divine drink. There are lots of very interested facts about wine that will make even those that are tea-total, want to start enjoying wine. For example, did you know?

- Wine has almost the same amount of calories as grape juice of the same size.

- With time, red wines become lighter, while white grow darker.

- An average number of grape berries needed for a bottle of wine is 600.

- In Utah, USA, it is forbidden to drink wine during wine tasting.

- Corks weren't used in France until the mid-17th century. Instead, rugs covered in oil were used.

- Bubbles in Champaign were considered a bad thing, earlier in history.

- The word "toasting" actually does come from toast, brown bread. The reason is that Romans used to toast with a bit of brad dipped in wine.

- In France, there was a saying that the best Champaign glasses were of the size of Marie Antoinette's breast.

- Pliny the Elder is the father of the phrase "in vino veritas".

- The year 121BC marks the beginning of Roman wine era as because of the good grape harvest, Roman wines became more popular than Greek wines.

- In the Middle Ages, wine was sometimes used as currency.

- Ancient Egyptians thought of wine as a gift from the God Osiris.

- In Armenia, there is a legend that the first vineyards on Earth were planted by Noah in their country.

- According to a Persian legend, wine was first made in the area that is nowadays Iran. It says that the wife of a Persian ruler accidentally drank sour grape juice and got drunk, which she liked a lot.

- Blanc de Noar are those white wines that were made from red grape.

- There are over 400 oak sorts on the planet, of which only 20 are used for making wine barrels. A single barrel takes about 5% of the total oak tree.

- An average age of the French oak trees cut down for wine barrel production, is 170 years.

- During the Tutankhamen era in the Ancient Egypt, ordinary people only drank beer, while the ruling class drank wine.

- When a Viking called Leif Erikson landed in North America in 1001AD, he was so impressed with wild vines that were growing there that he named the country Vinland (Wineland).

- When Vesuvius covered the whole city of Pompeii in ash, it also covered over 200 wine bars.

- There are so many chemical compounds in wine that it is considered more complex liquid than blood.

- The most common grape variety for wine production is Airen. There are vineyards of this sort in central Spain, covering an area of almost one million acres.

- Beaujolais Nouveau, the young wine, cannot be sold before third of November of the following year.

- Wine is often called the drink of the Gods, but the only sort of wine that was called after a deity is Sangiovese, meaning the blood of Job.

- Egg whites, bull blood and gelatin, used to be used for wine filtration.

- Portugal is the world's biggest producer of cork. Almost 90% of cork used in the US comes from Portugal.

- Bordeaux is a synonym for red wine, but before 1970, this French region produced more white wine.

- Champaign glass will create more bubbles if it's inside surface is not smooth.

- The speed of a Champaign cork, when opening a bottle, is about 46 km/h.

- Every year the beginning of grape harvesting is announced by the French authorities. It is forbidden to start harvesting before that.

- A collector of wine labels is called vintitulis.

- In the Ancient Greece, men older than 40 were allowed to drink as many wine as they wanted. Those younger were controlled, while famous philosopher Plato thought that men younger than 18 should be banned for drinking wine.

- According to a tale, the bishop of Tour discovered the importance of grape pruning, when his donkey, which he left unattended, eat bits of vines. When the bishop died, he was named the Saint Martin and became the protector of drunken people.

- In the late Middle Ages, ill people in Germany were treated with 7 liters of wine per day.

- The best way to remove red wine stains is to spill white wine over it. The white wine will neutralize the color of the red wine, thus saving your clothes.

- The record for the longest flight of a Champaign cork is 53.32 meters.

- There are around 49 million bubbles in every bottle of Champaign.

- The oldest collection of exquisite wines is located on the bottom of the Atlantic Ocean – in Titanic. When it sank, the biggest ship of the time took a huge collection of the finest wines with it. It is believed that the most of the bottles are not damaged. Actually, some of them were salvaged recently, all of which were in perfect conditions.

- Despite being a sort of a white wine, most of French Champaign sorts are made from grapes used for red wine production – Pinot Noar and Pinot Meunier.

- About 115 million liters of wine were spilled during the 1906 San Francisco earthquake, which is one of the biggest catastrophes in the history of wine.

Finally, if you enjoyed this book, then I'd like to ask you for a favor, would you be kind enough to leave a review for this book on Amazon? It'd be greatly appreciated!

Thank you and good luck!

Printed in Great Britain
by Amazon.co.uk, Ltd.,
Marston Gate.